Chronicles Of The Kings Of Israel And Judah

Timeline And List Of The Kings Of Israel In Order

By
Chris Adkins

Visit Blog

http://www.livingabrightlifenow.com

Disclaimer Of Warranty / Limitations Of Liability

The author and publisher of this book and the accompanying materials have used their best efforts to accurately represent this product and its potential in preparing this book/program. The author and publisher make no representation or warranties with respect to the accuracy, applicability, fitness, or completeness of the contents of this book/program. The information contained in this book is strictly for informational and/or educational purposes and should serve only as a general guide and not as the ultimate source of subject information. The author and publisher shall in no event be held liable or responsible to any person, party, or entity regarding any direct, indirect, punitive, special, incidental or other consequential damages or loss arising directly or indirectly from any use of this material, and without warranties. ***I am not a lawyer***. This information is provided and sold with the knowledge that the author and publisher do not offer any legal or other professional advice. As always, if you have any specific questions, the advice of a competent legal, tax, accounting, financial, medical, or other appropriately qualified professional should be sought. The author and publisher do not warrant the performance, effectiveness or applicability of any sites listed or linked to in this book or any accompanying materials. All links are for information purposes only and are not warranted for content, accuracy or any other implied or explicit purpose.

Copyright © 2014 by Chris Adkins

All rights reserved. No material in this book may be reproduced, transmitted, or utilized in any form or by any means, electronic or mechanical, including photocopying, recording, or by any information storage and retrieval system, without permission from the author.

About The Author – Chris Adkins

Inventor and Author, Formal Education - Psychology

Specializing in helping individuals experience joy, wholeness and healing, peace of mind, and comfort for the spirit, soul, and body.

With past health challenges and questions, this began her quest to find answers. Her journey has led to an exhaustive study of bible scripture and self-help, seeking the 'genuine truth' and not just opinions or suggestions disguised as truth. She had found that the scripture is the inspired word of God, which led her to the scripture 'I am the way and the truth and the life' (John 14:6). She enjoys a tranquil peace now, and knows where to seek to maintain her comfort, health and peace of mind.

The Author's Mission:

My mission in life is not merely to survive, but to thrive; and to do so with some passion, some compassion, some humor and some style. - Dr. Maya Angelou

Table Of Contents

Disclaimer Of Warranty/Limitations Of Liability

About The Author – Chris Adkins

Introduction

Chapter 1 - The United Kingdom Of Israel (3 Kings)

Chapter 2 - Explanation For The United Kingdom Of Israel Splitting Into Southern And Northern Kingdoms

Chapter 3 - The Southern Kingdom Of Israel (The 20 Kings Of Judah) (The Royal Line of Jesus)

Chapter 4 - The Remaining 12 Generations Of The Royal Line Of Jesus (Traced Through

Joseph's Lineage) Who Were Not Kings

Chapter 5 - The Northern Kingdom Of Israel (The 19 Kings Of Israel)

Conclusion

Bible References

Check Out My Other Books On Amazon

Introduction

Hello, Chris Adkins here and I offer you a warm welcome and thank you for your interest in this book. You are about to discover the timeline and history of the Kings of Israel and Judah. You will also learn about the Northern and Southern Kingdoms.

In fact, this book gives you the answers to these important questions:

- Who is the first King of Israel?

- Who is the last King of Israel?

- Who is the youngest King of Israel?

- Who was David, the King of Israel?

- Who are the Kings of Israel in chronological order?

- And much, much more!

I've created this book to give you insight into God's Word about the lives of the Kings of Israel and Judah. My goal was to find all the scriptures pertaining to the Kings. It was essential for me to start in the beginning, to truly understand and grasp the entire meaningful life experience of Jesus, who paid the ultimate epic price for ALL of us! I received a much greater knowledge of Jesus and our blood covenant by studying the royal line of Jesus and the lineage of the Kings of Israel. To the best of my knowledge, this study of the lineage is accurate.

I hope you enjoy this book, I believe there's a lot of very good information to take in, such as the where the Kings were born, how many years they reigned, and the meaning of their names. You can learn in minutes what it took me upon hours and hours to learn. You are about to begin and explore a historical journey through the kings, from the first human king and ending with The King of Kings.

Make sure to read the entire book.

Enjoy!

Chris Adkins

Chapter 1 – The United Kingdom Of Israel

(3 Kings)

King Saul - asked (of God)

The FIRST King of Israel

Born in Gibeon - of the tribe of Benjamin

Reigned 2 years - 1 Samuel 13:1

B.C. 1096-1056 is recorded

1 Samuel 10:1-16, 1 Samuel 11:15, 1 Samuel 31:13, 1 Chronicles 10:1-14

King David – well beloved

The SECOND King of Israel

Born in Bethlehem - of the tribe of Judah

Reigned 40 years - 2 Samuel 4:4-5

B.C. 1086-1016 is recorded

2 Samuel 2:4, 1 Kings 2:11, 1 Chronicles 11-29

King Solomon – peace

The THIRD King of Israel

Born in Jerusalem - of the tribe of Judah

Reigned 40 years - 1 Kings 11:41-43

Of Joseph's lineage - Matthew 1:6-16

B.C. 1033-975 is recorded

1 Kings 1:39, 1 Kings 2:12, 1 Kings 11:43,
1 Chronicles 29:22-25, 2 Chronicles 1-9

Chapter 2 – Explanation For The United Kingdom Of Israel Splitting Into Southern And Northern Kingdoms

In the time of King Solomon's reign, The Lord commanded the Israelite's not to follow after other gods, and not to go into certain nations, neither to let those nations come in. But, King Solomon sinned and turned his heart away from The Lord in his old age, because he loved many of the women who were of those very nations. Solomon clung unto these in love, having 700 wives, princesses, and 300 concubines. His wives turned his heart from God and toward other gods. So, Solomon did evil in the sight of The Lord and did not follow after The Lord, as David his father did. The Lord was angry with

Solomon, which had appeared unto him twice and had commanded him that he should not go after other gods. Solomon did not heed God's warnings, and he had forsaken God and worshiped other gods. Therefore, The Lord rended the Kingdom from out of the hand of Solomon's son, Rehoboam. However, God would not tear away all the Kingdom for David's sake and for the sake of Jerusalem. So, God gave one tribe to Rehoboam, so that David, God's servant, may always have a Light before God in Jerusalem, the city where God had chosen out of all the Tribes of Israel to put His name. Instead, the Kingdom was given to his servant Jeroboam, consisting of ten tribes.

It came to pass, Solomon died and his son Rehoboam reigned in his stead. Jeroboam and all the congregation came to King Rehoboam, to make the heavy yoke which his father put on them lighter. King Rehoboam answered the people roughly and harkened not unto the people; for the cause was from The Lord, that He might perform His saying, which The Lord spoke by Ahijah the prophet unto Jeroboam. Therefore, Israel rebelled against the house of David, and King Rehoboam fled to Jerusalem. There was none that followed the house of David, but the Tribe of Judah only.

King Rehoboam assembled all the House of Judah in Jerusalem with the Tribe of Benjamin, which became known as (The Southern Kingdom of Israel), and Israel sent and called Jeroboam unto the congregation and made him King over all Israel, which became known as (The Northern Kingdom of Israel). There was war between Rehoboam and Jeroboam all their days. (1 Kings 11-14)

Chapter 3 – The Southern Kingdom Of Israel

(The 20 Kings Of Judah)
(The Royal Line Of Jesus)

King Rehoboam - the people are enlarged

The **FIRST** King of Judah

Reigned 17 years - 1 Kings 14:21

B.C. 975 is recorded

1 Kings 12:11, 1 Kings 12:21-24, 1 Kings 14:29-31, 2 Chronicles 10-12

King Abijam - Jehovah is Father

Reigned 3 years - 1 Kings 15:2

B.C. - is unknown

1 Kings 15:1-8, 2 Chronicles 13:1-22

King Asa – physician

Reigned 41 years - 2 Chronicles 16:13

B.C. 914 is recorded

1 Kings 15:9-24, 2 Chronicles 14:1,
2 Chronicles 15:1-19, 2 Chronicles 16:1-14

King Jehoshaphat - Jehovah has judged

Reigned 25 years - 1 Kings 22:42

B.C. 900 is recorded

1 Kings 15:24, 1 Kings 22:41-50, 2 Chronicles 17-20

King Jehoram - Jehovah is high

Reigned 8 years - 2 Kings 8:16-17

B.C. 893-885 is recorded

2 Kings 8:16-24, 2 Chronicles 21:1-20

King Ahaziah - Jehovah has grasped

Succeeded his father Jehoram

Reigned 1 year - 2 Chronicles 22:2

B.C. 884 is recorded

2 Kings 8:25-29, 2 Kings 9:27-28, 2 Chronicles 22:1-9

King Athaliah - Jehovah is exalted

Mother of Ahaziah **(Queen reigns)**

Usurped throne for 6 years - 2 Kings 11:3

B.C. 884 is recorded

2 Kings 11:1-21, 2 Chronicles 22:10-12,
2 Chronicles 23:1-21

King Joash - Jehovah has given

Succeeded his father Ahaziah

Reigned 40 years - 2 Kings 12:1

B.C. 850 is recorded

2 Kings 11:1-3, 2 Kings 11:21, 2 Kings 12:1-21,
2 Chronicles 24:1-27

King Amaziah - Jehovah is strong

Succeeded his father Joash

Reigned 29 years - 2 Kings 14:2

B.C. 839 is recorded

2 Kings 12:21, 2 Kings 14:1-20, 1 Chronicles 3:12, 2 Chronicles 25:1-28

King Azariah - Jehovah has helped

Succeeded his father

Reigned 52 years - 2 Kings 15:1-2

B.C. 809 is recorded

2 Kings 14:21, 2 Kings 15:1-26, 1 Chronicles 3:12, 2 Chronicles 26:1-23

King Jotham - Jehovah is perfect

Succeeded his father Azariah

Reigned 16 years - 2 Kings 15:33

B.C. 750 is recorded

2 Kings 15:7, 2 Kings 15:32-38, 1 Chronicles 3:12, 1 Chronicles 27:1-9

King Ahaz - he has grasped

Succeeded his father Jotham

Reigned 16 years - 2 Kings 16:1-2

B.C. 740-724 is recorded

2 Kings 15:38, 2 Kings 16:1-20, 2 Chronicles 28:1-27

King Hezekiah - Jehovah strengthens

Succeeded his father Ahaz

Reigned 29 years - 2 Kings 18:2

B.C. 724-697 is recorded

2 Kings 16:20, 2 Kings 18-20,
2 Chronicles 29-32

King Manasseh - making to forget

Succeeded his father Hezekiah

Reigned 55 years - 2 Kings 21:1

B.C. 680 is recorded

2 Kings 21:1-18, 2 Chronicles 32:33,
2 Chronicles 33:1-20

King Amon - master workman

Reigned 2 years - 2 Kings 21:1

B.C. 643 is recorded

2 Kings 21:18-26, 2 Chronicles 33:21-25

King Josiah - Jehovah heals

Succeeded his father Amon

Reigned 31 years - 2 Kings 22:1

B.C. 642-611 is recorded

1 Kings 13:1-2, 2 Kings 22-23, 2 Chronicles 34-35, Jeremiah 22:15-18

King Jehoahaz - Jehovah has taken hold of

Succeeded his father Josiah

Reigned 3 months - 2 Kings 23:31

Deposed by Pharaoh Necho

B.C. 610 is recorded

2 Kings 23:30-34, 1 Chronicles 3:15,
2 Chronicles 36:1-4

King Jehoiakim - Jehovah raises up

Son of King Josiah - brother of Jehoahaz

Succeeded his brother Jehoahaz

Reigned 11 years - 2 Chronicles 36:5

B.C. 610-600 is recorded

2 Kings 23:34-37, 2 Kings 24:1-7, 1 Chronicles 3:15-16, 2 Chronicles 36:1-8, Jeremiah 1:3, Jeremiah 22, Jeremiah 24-28, Jeremiah 35-37

King Jehoiachin - Jehovah establishes

Succeeded his father Jehoiakim

Set on the throne by Nebuchadnezzar

Reigned 3 months - 2 Kings 24:8

B.C. 600 is recorded

2 Kings 24:8-16, 2 Kings 25:27-30, 2 Chronicles 36:8-10, Jeremiah 52:31-34

King Zedekiah - Jehovah is righteousness

Uncle and successor of Jehoiachin

Reigned 11 years - 2 Kings 24:18

B.C. 588 is recorded

2 Kings 24:17-20, 2 Kings 25:1-7, 2 Chronicles 36:11-13, Jeremiah 34:1-22, Jeremiah 37-39, Ezekiel 17:11-21

Chapter 4 – The Remaining 12 Generations Of The Royal Line Of Jesus (Traced Through Joseph's Lineage) Who Were Not Kings

Salathiel - Shealtiel - I have asked God

Ancestor of Jesus - Matthew 1:12

Son of King Jeconiah - 1 Chronicles 3:17

Salethial begat a son- Zorobabel - Matthew 1:12

B.C. 580 is recorded

Zorobabel - Zerubbabel - Seed of Babel

Ancestor of Jesus - Matthew 1:12-13

Descendent of David - 1 Chronicles 3:19

Chosen by God as the one to renew His

covenant to David's prophetic line -Haggai 2:20-23, 2 Samuel 7:12-16

Called by God to rebuild the temple - Haggai 1:1-15

Rebuilds the temple - Zechariah 4:1-14

Leader of Jewish exiles - Nehemiah 7:6-7

Restores worship in Jerusalem - Ezra 3:1-8

Zorobabel begat a son- Abiud - Matthew 1:13

Abiud - Abihud - The Father is Majesty

Ancestor of Jesus - Matthew 1:13

Eliakim - God will establish

Ancestor of Jesus - Matthew 1:13

Azor - Helper

Ancestor of Jesus - Matthew 1:14

Sadoc - Righteous

Ancestor of Jesus - Matthew 1:14

Achim - Woes

Ancestor of Jesus - Matthew 1:14

Eliud - God is Mighty

Ancestor of Jesus - Matthew 1:15

Eleazar - God has helped

Ancestor of Jesus - Matthew 1:15

Matthan - Gift

Ancestor of Jesus - Matthew 1:15

Jacob - Supplanter

Ancestor of Jesus - Matthew 1:15-16

Father of Joseph the Husband of Mary, of whom was born Jesus, who is called Christ - Matthew 1:15-16

Joseph - May He (Jehovah) add –

Husband of Mary Jesus' Mother - Matthew 1:16

With Mary at Jesus' Birth - Luke 2:16

So all the generations from Abraham to David are fourteen generations; and from David until the carrying away into Babylon are fourteen generations; and from the carrying away into Babylon unto Christ are fourteen generations. (Matthew 1:17)

Chapter 5 – The Northern Kingdom Of Israel

(The 19 Kings Of Israel)

Jeroboam - May the people increase

The **FIRST** King of the ten tribes of Israel

Reigned 22 years - 1 Kings 14:20

B.C. 970 is recorded

1 Kings 12:20, 1 Kings 12:25-33, 1 Kings 13:1-34, 1 Kings 14:1-20, 2 Chronicles 13:20

Nadab - Willing, liberal

Succeeded his father Jeroboam

Reigned 2 years - 1 Kings 15:25

B.C. 954 is recorded

1 Kings 14:20, 1 Kings 15:25-32

Baasha - Boldness

Son of Ahijah - Of the house of Issachar

Gained throne by murder

Reigned 24 years - 1 Kings 15:33

B.C. 953 is recorded

1 Kings 15:16-34, 1 Kings 16:1-13,
2 Chronicles 16:1-6, Jeremiah 41:9

Elah - An oak

Succeeded his father Baasha

Reigned 2 years - 1 Kings 16:8

B.C. 930 is recorded

1 Kings 16:6-14

Zimri - Pertaining to an antelope, celebrated

Servant of Elah - Gained throne by murder

Reigned 7 days - 1 Kings 16:15

B.C. 929 is recorded

1 Kings 16:8-20, 2 Kings 9:31

Omri - Jehovah apportions

All Israel made Omri Captain of the Host -

And the city was taken

Reigned 12 years - 1 Kings 16:23

B.C. 929-907 is recorded

1 Kings 16:16-28, 2 Kings 8:26, 2 Chronicles 22:2, Micah 6:16

Ahab - Father's brother

Succeeded his father Omri as **SEVENTH** King

Reigned 22 years - 1 Kings 16:29

B.C. 919-897 is recorded

1 Kings 16-22, 2 Kings 8-10, 2 Chronicles 18:1-34, 2 Chronicles 21:6-13, 2 Chronicles 22:1-9, Micah 6:16

Ahaziah - Jehovah has grasped

Succeeded his father Ahab as **EIGHTH** King

Reigned 2 years - 1 Kings 22:51

B.C. 896-895 is recorded

1 Kings 22:40-53, 2 Kings 1:2-18, 1 Chronicles 3:11, 2 Chronicles 20:35-37

Jehoram - Jehovah is high

Son of Ahab, brother of Ahaziah reigned in his stead

Because Ahaziah had no son

Reigned 12 years - 2 Kings 3:1

B.C. 896-884 is recorded

2 Kings 1:17, 2 Kings 3:1-27, 2 Kings 5:1-27, 2 Kings 6:8-23, 2 Kings 8:16-29, 2 Kings 9:14-29, 2 Chronicles 22:5-7

Jehu - Jehovah is He

Anointed by Elijah as King

Reigned 28 years - 2 Kings 10:36

B.C. 884-856 is recorded

1 Kings 19:16-17, 2 Kings 9-10, 2 Kings 15:12, 2 Chronicles 22:7-9, 2 Chronicles 25:17, Hosea 1:4

Jehoahaz - Jehovah has taken hold of

Succeeded his father Jehu

Reigned 17 years - 2 Kings 13:1

B.C. 885 is recorded

2 Kings 10:35, 2 Kings 13:1-9

Jehoash - Jehovah has given

Succeeded his father Jehoahaz

Reigned 16 years - 2 Kings 13:10

B.C. 840 is recorded

2 Kings 13:9-25, 2 Chronicles 25:17-25

Jeroboam II - May the people increase

Succeeded his father Jehoash

Reigned 41 years - 2 Kings 14:23

B.C. 825 is recorded

2 Kings 13:13, 2 Kings 14:16, 2 Kings 14:23-29, 1 Chronicles 5:17, Amos 1:1, Amos 7:9-11

Zechariah - Jehovah remembers

Succeeded his father Jeroboam II

Reigned 6 months - 2 Kings 15:8

B.C. 773 is recorded

2 Kings 14:29, 2 Kings 15:8-12

Shallum - Recompense

Son of Jabesh

Gained throne by murder

Reigned 1 month - 2 Kings 15:13

B.C. 772 is recorded

2 Kings 15:10-15

Menahem - Comforter

Son of Gadi

Gained throne by murder

Reigned 10 years - 2 Kings 15:17

B.C. 761 is recorded

2 Kings 15:14-22

Pekahiah - Jehovah has opened (the eyes)

Succeeded his father Menahem

Reigned 2 years - 2 Kings 15:23

B.C. 761 is recorded

2 Kings 15:22-26

Pekah - Opening (of the eye)

An officer of Pekahiah

Son of Remaliah

Usurped Israel's throne

Reigned 20 years - 2 Kings 15:27

B.C. 759-739 is recorded

2 Kings 15:25-31, Isaiah 7:1-9, 2 Kings 16:1-5, 2 Chronicles 28:6

Hoshea - Save

The **NINETEENTH** last and best King of Israel

Son of Elah

Usurped Israel's throne

Reigned 9 years - 2 Kings 17:1

B.C. 729-720 is recorded

2 Kings 15:30, 2 Kings 17:1-6, 2 Kings 18:9-10

Conclusion

Thank you again for purchasing this book!
I hope this book was able to help you achieve a better understanding into the Kings of Israel.

Thank you for your time. I wish you the best of luck!

Chris Adkins

http://www.livingabrightlifenow.com

Bible References

Parallel Bible (KJV - AMP)

The New Strong's Exhaustive Concordance Of The Bible

Young's Analytical Concordance Of The Bible

Vine's Expository Dictionary Of The Bible

Check Out My Other Books On Amazon

If you are interested, you will find other 'Religion & Spirituality' books that are popular on Amazon and Kindle as well. Simply copy and paste the book title into the search bar on Amazon dot Com.
Alternatively, you can visit my author page on Amazon to see other work done by me.

https://www.amazon.com/author/cadkins

The Names Of God From A To Z Explained: Exploring God's Character With 1000+ Names Of God And Their Meanings ~ By Chris Adkins

List Of 'I AM' Affirmations ~ By Chris Adkins

Healing Scriptures From Genesis To Revelation: 300 Healing Bible Verses On The Proven Healing Promises From God's Word ~ By Chris Adkins

Chronicles Of The Kings Of Israel And Judah: Timeline And List Of The Kings Of Israel In Order ~ By Chris Adkins

The Genealogy Of Jesus In The Bible: A Chronological List Of The Genealogy Of Jesus Through Mary ~ By Chris Adkins

Healing Scriptures For A Broken Heart: Experience Emotional Healing And Healing The Wounds Of The Past ~ By Chris Adkins

[Grieving A Loss: Scriptures On Grief Recovery And Coping With Grief And Loss ~ By Chris Adkins](#)

[Forgiven: Scriptures On Forgiveness And Proven Second Chances ~ By Chris Adkins](#)

[Life Or Death: Salvation By Grace Scriptures And Holy Spirit Scriptures To Live By ~ By Chris Adkins](#)